LEADING YOUR KIDS TO CHRIST

30 DAYS TO PREPARE YOUR HEART

FAMILY
Christian Stores

FAMILY CHRISTIAN STORES
Grand Rapids, MI 49530

The quoted ideas expressed in this book (but not scripture verses) are not, in all cases, exact quotations, as some have been edited for clarity and brevity. In all cases, the author has attempted to maintain the speaker's original intent. In some cases, quoted material for this book was obtained from secondary sources, primarily print media. While every effort was made to ensure the accuracy of these sources, the accuracy cannot be guaranteed. For additions, deletions, corrections or clarifications in future editions of this text, please write FAMILY CHRISTIAN STORES.

Cover Design Kim Russell / Wahoo Designs
Page Layout by Bart Dawson

ISBN 978-1-60587-190-5

Printed in the United States of America

THE REAL FAITH SERIES

LEADING YOUR KIDS TO CHRIST

30 DAYS TO PREPARE YOUR HEART

TABLE OF CONTENTS

INTRODUCTION

IT'S A PROCESS

As a Christian parent, you have many responsibilities. But no parental duty is more important than that of leading your child to Christ. And the ideas in this book can be helpful.

This text is divided into 30 lessons, one for each day of the month. But the job of helping your child build a lasting relationship with Jesus is a lengthy process, not a 30-day crash course. So here's a suggestion: read a lesson each day for a month and during that time, think carefully about each day's message and its implications for your child. Then, when you've completed this text, refer back to it often, paying careful attention to the personal notes you've made at the end of each chapter. When you do, you'll discover that your child's spiritual journey is intertwined with your own: As your youngster's relationship with the Savior matures, so, too, will yours.

If you have been touched by Christ's love and His grace, then you know the joy that He has brought into your own life. Now it's your turn to share His message with the boy or girl whom He has entrusted to your care. Happy reading! And may God richly bless you and your family now and forever.

Part I

PREPARING YOURSELF

You can't lead your child on a spiritual journey you're not willing to take yourself. So the first step in leading your child to Christ is, not surprisingly, to form your own life-altering relationship with Him. And that means accepting Jesus as your personal Savior. The first eight lessons of this text are intended to help you examine your own faith as you prepare for future discussions with your youngster.

Chapter 1

RECOGNIZING YOUR PARENTAL RESPONSIBILITIES

Therefore you shall lay up these words of mine
in your heart and in your soul . . . .
You shall teach them to your children,
speaking of them when you sit in your house,
when you walk by the way, when you lie down,
and when you rise up.
Deuteronomy 11:18-19 NKJV

TODAY'S BIG IDEA

As a Christian parent, you have many important responsibilities. But no responsibility is more important than your duty, as a parent, to lead your child to Christ.

If you're a parent in our 21st-century world, you need keen insight, prudent foresight, and sharp eyesight. But that's not all. You also need discipline, patience, prayer, and a willingness to teach. Of all these parental duties, none can compare with the responsibility of teaching your child about Jesus.

Are you genuinely excited about the opportunity to talk to your youngster about Christ? Hopefully so, because your child desperately needs to hear the Good News of God's Son—and your child deserves to hear that story from you.

When you begin the process of leading your child to Christ—the process of walking with and talking about Jesus every day—you'll be building a spiritual legacy for generations to come. So, if you haven't already done so, start the conversation about God's Son today. Don't restrict these conversations to Sunday mornings: Talk about Jesus seven days a week. And remember that your most enduring lessons are not necessarily the ones you teach with words; they are the lessons you teach by example. When you obey God's commandments, trust His promises, and follow in the footsteps of His Son, your life will serve as an enduring example to your children.

MORE FROM GOD'S WORD ABOUT JESUS

The next day John saw Jesus coming toward him and said, "Here is the Lamb of God, who takes away the sin of the world!"

John 1:29 Holman CSB

I am the door. If anyone enters by Me, he will be saved.

John 10:9 NKJV

I have come as a light into the world, so that everyone who believes in Me would not remain in darkness.

John 12:46 Holman CSB

I am the true vine, and My Father is the vineyard keeper. Every branch in Me that does not produce fruit He removes, and He prunes every branch that produces fruit so that it will produce more fruit.

John 15:1-2 Holman CSB

Jesus Christ is the same yesterday, today, and forever.

Hebrews 13:8 Holman CSB

MORE IMPORTANT IDEAS ABOUT CHRIST'S LOVE

Begin very early to instruct a child on the true values of life: love for all mankind, kindness, integrity, trustworthiness, truthfulness, and devotion to God.

James Dobson

The children taught me much as they were growing up: about themselves, about the world around them, about me, and especially about God.

Ruth Bell Graham

Never underestimate the power that comes when a parent pleads with God on behalf of a child.

Max Lucado

OUR CHILDREN BELONG TO GOD

Our children are not really our possessions; our youngsters are, in truth, God's children. They belong to Him, and He entrusts them to our care for a little while. And then, we must let them go.

WRITE DOWN YOUR IDEAS ABOUT . . .

What it means to be a Christian parent.

Chapter 2

Examine Your Own Faith

For I assure you: If you have faith the size of a mustard seed, you will tell this mountain, "Move from here to there," and it will move. Nothing will be impossible for you.

Matthew 17:20 Holman CSB

TODAY'S BIG IDEA

Your child's faith will be a direct reflection of your faith. If you want your child's faith to be strong, your faith should be strong, too.

Jesus loves your family so much that He endured unspeakable humiliation and suffering for you and your loved ones. How will you respond to Christ's sacrifice? Will you take up His cross and follow Him, or will you choose another path? When you place your hopes squarely at the foot of the cross—and when you place Jesus squarely at the center of your home life—you will be blessed.

The 19th-century writer Hannah Whitall Smith observed, "The crucial question for each of us is this: What do you think of Jesus, and do you yet have a personal acquaintance with Him?" This question applies not only to you, but also to your clan.

Thomas Brooks spoke for believers of every generation when he observed, "Christ is the sun, and all the watches of our lives should be set by the dial of his motion." Christ, indeed, is the ultimate Savior of mankind and the personal Savior of those who believe in Him. As His servants, we should place Him at the very center of our lives and at the center of our households. When we do, we are blessed today, tomorrow, and throughout eternity.

Are you a parent whose faith is evident for all to see? Do you trust God's promises without reservation, or do you question His promises without hesitation? Are you willing to walk with Christ and talk about Him to your youngster? The answer to these questions will have a direct impact on your ability to help your child grow spiritually and emotionally.

Jesus taught His disciples that if they had faith, they could move mountains. You can, too, and so can your family. But you must have faith. So today and every day, trust your Heavenly Father, praise the sacrifice of His Son . . . and then let the mountain-moving begin.

Faith means believing in advance
what will only make sense in reverse.
Philip Yancey

MORE FROM GOD'S WORD ABOUT FAITH

Now faith is the reality of what is hoped for, the proof of what is not seen.

Hebrews 11:1 Holman CSB

For we walk by faith, not by sight.

2 Corinthians 5:7 Holman CSB

Now without faith it is impossible to please God, for the one who draws near to Him must believe that He exists and rewards those who seek Him.

Hebrews 11:6 Holman CSB

If you do not stand firm in your faith, then you will not stand at all.

Isaiah 7:9 Holman CSB

Jesus said, "Because you have seen Me, you have believed. Blessed are those who believe without seeing."

John 20:29 Holman CSB

MORE IMPORTANT IDEAS ABOUT THE POWER OF FAITH

Your children learn more of your faith during the bad times than they do during the good times.

Beverly LaHaye

Just as our faith strengthens our prayer life, so do our prayers deepen our faith. Let us pray often, starting today, for a deeper, more powerful faith.

Shirley Dobson

Faith never knows where it is being led, but it loves the One who is leading.

Oswald Chambers

DON'T BE EMBARRASSED TO DISCUSS YOUR FAITH

You need not have attended seminary to have worthwhile opinions about your faith. Express those opinions, especially to your children; your kids need to know where you stand.

WRITE DOWN YOUR IDEAS ABOUT . . .

What your faith means to you.

Chapter 3

Asking God to Guide Your Steps

So I say to you, keep asking, and it will be given to you. Keep searching, and you will find. Keep knocking, and the door will be opened to you.

Luke 11:9 Holman CSB

TODAY'S BIG IDEA

If you need help communicating with your child, ask God for His help in finding the right words to say. When you ask Him, sincerely and often, He will answer your prayers.

Jesus made it clear to His disciples: they should petition God to meet their needs. So should you. If you're a parent who's trying to find the right words to say or the right lessons to teach, you should ask God for His guidance early and often.

Genuine, heartfelt prayer can produce powerful changes in your life, in your world, and in your family. And when you lift up your heart to God sincerely and often, you open yourself to a never-ending source of divine wisdom and infinite love. Simply put, prayer works. Yet far too many people are too timid or too pessimistic to ask God to do big things. Please don't count yourself among their number.

God can do great things through you if you have the courage to ask Him (and the determination to keep asking Him). He has promised that when you ask for His help, He will not withhold it. So ask. Ask Him to meet the needs of your day and the needs of your family. Ask Him to lead you, to protect you, and to correct you. Then, trust the answers He gives.

God stands at the door and waits. When you knock, He opens. When you ask, He answers. Your task, of course, is to seek His guidance prayerfully, confidently, and often.

MORE FROM GOD'S WORD ABOUT ASKING GOD

If you remain in Me and My words remain in you, ask whatever you want and it will be done for you.

John 15:7 Holman CSB

What father among you, if his son asks for a fish, will, instead of a fish, give him a snake? Or if he asks for an egg, will give him a scorpion? If you then, who are evil, know how to give good gifts to your children, how much more will the heavenly Father give the Holy Spirit to those who ask Him?

Luke 11:11-13 Holman CSB

And in that day you will ask Me nothing. Most assuredly, I say to you, whatever you ask the Father in My name He will give you. Until now you have asked nothing in My name. Ask, and you will receive, that your joy may be full.

John 16:23-24 NKJV

Don't worry about anything, but in everything, through prayer and petition with thanksgiving, let your requests be made known to God.

Philippians 4:6 Holman CSB

You do not have because you do not ask.

James 4:2 Holman CSB

MORE IMPORTANT IDEAS ABOUT ASKING GOD

Some people think God does not like to be troubled with our constant asking. But, the way to trouble God is not to come at all.

D. L. Moody

Don't be afraid to ask your heavenly Father for anything you need. Indeed, nothing is too small for God's attention or too great for his power.

Dennis Swanberg

When will we realize that we're not troubling God with our questions and concerns? His heart is open to hear us—his touch nearer than our next thought—as if no one in the world existed but us. Our very personal God wants to hear from us personally.

Gigi Graham Tchividjian

PARENTS SHOULD ASK FOR HELP, TOO

If you need help, ask. And remember this: God is listening, and He wants to help you right now.

WRITE DOWN YOUR IDEAS ABOUT . . .

The importance of asking God for His blessings and His help.

Chapter 4

PRAYING FOR YOUR CHILDREN

I have no greater joy than this:
to hear that my children are
walking in the truth.
3 John 1:4 Holman CSB

TODAY'S BIG IDEA

Absolutely no parental duty is more important than the duty of praying for your child.

The power of prayer: these words are so familiar, yet sometimes we forget what they mean. Prayer is a powerful tool for communicating with our Creator; it is an opportunity to commune with the Giver of all things good. Prayer is not a thing to be taken lightly or to be used infrequently.

Far too many parents, feeling swamped by the demands of providing for their families, lose sight of God's presence in their lives. Instead of turning to Him for guidance and for comfort, they depend, instead, upon their own limited resources. To do so is a profound mistake.

In his first letter to the Thessalonians, Paul wrote, "Rejoice evermore. Pray without ceasing. In every thing give thanks: for this is the will of God in Christ Jesus concerning you" (5:17-18 KJV). Paul's words should have special meaning to you, a Christian parent who's determined to lead your child to Christ.

So today, instead of turning things over in your mind, turn them over to God in prayer. Instead of worrying about your decisions, trust God to help you make them. Today, pray constantly about things great and small—and pray for the spiritual well-being of your child. God is listening, and He wants to hear from you. Now.

It is a joy that God never abandons His children. He guides faithfully all who listen to His directions.

Corrie ten Boom

MORE FROM GOD'S WORD ABOUT PRAYER

The intense prayer of the righteous is very powerful.

James 5:16 Holman CSB

Let the words of my mouth and the meditation of my heart be acceptable in Your sight, O Lord, my strength and my Redeemer.

Psalm 19:14 NKJV

Yet He often withdrew to deserted places and prayed.

Luke 5:16 Holman CSB

Don't worry about anything, but in everything, through prayer and petition with thanksgiving, let your requests be made known to God.

Philippians 4:6 Holman CSB

Rejoice in hope; be patient in affliction; be persistent in prayer.

Romans 12:12 Holman CSB

MORE IMPORTANT IDEAS ABOUT PRAYER

Praying for our children is a noble task. There is nothing more special, more precious, than time that a parent spends struggling and pondering with God on behalf of a child.

Max Lucado

I'm a hundred and two years old, and I still pray for my children every day. I always have; I always will.

Marie T. Freeman

God's plan for our guidance is for us to grow gradually in wisdom before we get to the crossroads.

Bill Hybels

IT'S ALWAYS A GOOD TIME TO PRAY

Pray early and often. God is listening, and your children are watching.

WRITE DOWN YOUR IDEAS ABOUT . . .

The importance of praying for your children.

Chapter 5

Being a Proactive Parent

Unless the Lord builds a house,
its builders labor over it in vain;
unless the Lord watches over a city,
the watchman stays alert in vain.
Psalm 127:1 Holman CSB

TODAY'S BIG IDEA

When it comes to the job of teaching your youngster about Jesus, accountability begins with the person you see in the mirror. As a responsible Christian parent, you should tell the story of Jesus clearly, confidently, and often.

When it comes to the terribly important job of raising kids, far too many parents seem willing to "go with the flow." They assume (wrongly) that if they just do what comes naturally, their children will turn out just fine. As a result, far too many parents have, in essence, "subcontracted out" the job of raising their kids. They have left childrearing to "the experts" down at the local school system or—and this is a scary thought—to their child's peer group. Then, when these same parents discover that their youngsters have acquired some very bad habits, Mom and Dad are quick to blame anybody except the two people they see in the mirror.

As a responsible Christian parent, you must never be satisfied to be a reactive parent. And you must never outsource the crucial job of teaching your child about Jesus. Since you simply can't trust the world to teach your kid life's most important lessons, you must teach them yourself, and that means being proactive.

What does it mean to be a proactive parent? It means that you decide your child's spiritual curriculum, but it doesn't stop there. It also means that you decide what your young child watches on TV, and it means that you are aware of—and that you endorse—the overall environment of the school your youngster attends. Being a proactive parent also means that you pay particular attention to your child's playmates, and it means that you're intimately involved in the details of your youngster's life seven days a week, not just on weekends.

Being a proactive parent means that you'll probably be quite a bit stricter than many of the moms and dads on your block, and that's okay. After all, you're not trying to please your child's peers or their parents—you're trying to please God and share the Good News about His Son. And if that means that you don't follow the crowd, don't be worried or embarrassed . . . be grateful.

Let us look upon our children;
let us love them and train them as children
of the covenant and children of the promise.
These are the children of God.

Andrew Murray

MORE FROM GOD'S WORD ABOUT HONORING PARENTS

Honor your father and your mother so that you may have a long life in the land that the Lord your God is giving you.

Exodus 20:12 Holman CSB

Listen, my son, to your father's instruction and do not forsake your mother's teaching.

Proverbs 1:8 NIV

Let them first learn to do their duty to their own family and to repay their parents or grandparents. That pleases God.

1 Timothy 5:4 NCV

Fools reject their parents' correction, but anyone who accepts correction is wise.

Proverbs 15:5 NCV

Above all, put on love—the perfect bond of unity.

Colossians 3:14 Holman CSB

MORE IMPORTANT IDEAS ABOUT PARENTING

To be in your child's memories tomorrow, you have to be in their lives today!

Barbara Johnson

God didn't assign the spiritual upbringing of children to churches or Christian schools. He assigned it to parents.

Beth Moore

Children desperately need to know and hear in ways they understand and remember that they're loved and valued by Mom and Dad.

Gary Smalley & John Trent

BE A PARENT FIRST AND A FRIEND SECOND

At times, you'll be tempted to become "one of the boys" (or girls). Resist that temptation. Remember that your youngster has lots of friends but only a couple of parents. So whatever you do, don't abandon your paternal responsibilities . . . your child needs a parent more than a pal.

WRITE DOWN YOUR IDEAS ABOUT . . .

Parenting duties you need to accomplish right now.

Chapter 6

Asking God for Wisdom

Acquire wisdom—how much better it is than gold!
And acquire understanding—
it is preferable to silver.
Proverbs 16:16 Holman CSB

TODAY'S BIG IDEA

Simply put, wisdom starts with God. And if you want to convey real wisdom to your young child, you and your youngster should study God's Word together every day.

Do you seek wisdom for yourself and for your family? Of course you do. But as a savvy parent, you know that wisdom can be an elusive commodity in today's troubled world. In a society filled with temptations and distractions, it's easy for parent and child alike to stray far from the source of the ultimate wisdom: God's Holy Word.

When you begin a daily study of God's Word and live according to His commandments, you will become wise . . . in time. But don't expect to open your Bible today and be wise tomorrow. Wisdom is not like a mushroom; it does not spring up overnight. It is, instead, like an oak tree that starts as a tiny acorn, grows into a sapling, and eventually reaches up to the sky, tall and strong.

Today and every day, as a way of understanding God's plan for your life—and as a way of guiding your child toward Christ—study the Bible and live by it. When you do, you will accumulate a storehouse of wisdom that will enrich your own life and the lives of your family members, your friends, and the world.

MORE FROM GOD'S WORD ABOUT WISDOM

The fear of the Lord is the beginning of wisdom; a good understanding have all those who do His commandments. His praise endures forever.

Psalm 111:10 NKJV

So teach us to number our days, that we may gain a heart of wisdom.

Psalm 90:12 NKJV

A wise man will hear and increase learning, and a man of understanding will attain wise counsel.

Proverbs 1:5 NKJV

Therefore, everyone who hears these words of Mine and acts on them will be like a sensible man who built his house on the rock. The rain fell, the rivers rose, and the winds blew and pounded that house. Yet it didn't collapse, because its foundation was on the rock.

Matthew 7:24–25 Holman CSB

MORE IMPORTANT IDEAS ABOUT WISDOM

Hold your children before the Lord in fervent prayer throughout their years at home. There is no other source of confidence and wisdom in parenting. The God who made your children will hear your petitions. He has promised to do so.

James Dobson

If we neglect the Bible, we cannot expect to benefit from the wisdom and direction that result from knowing God's Word.

Vonette Bright

WHERE WISDOM BEGINS

Being a wise parent requires more than knowledge. Knowledge comes from text books, but wisdom comes from God. Wisdom begins with a thorough understanding of God's moral order, the eternal truths that are found in God's Holy Word.

WRITE DOWN YOUR IDEAS ABOUT . . .

Ways that God's wisdom differs from society's "wisdom."

Chapter 7

SEEING YOUR CHILD AS GOD'S GIFT TO YOU

Children are a gift from the LORD;
they are a reward from him.
Children born to a young man are like
sharp arrows in a warrior's hands.
Psalm 127:3-4 NLT

TODAY'S BIG IDEA

It's hard work being a responsible parent, but the rewards always outweigh the costs. Simply put, your youngster is a marvelous gift from God. And, your opportunity to be a parent is yet another gift, for which you should give thanks.

As a parent, you are keenly aware that God has entrusted you with a priceless treasure from above: your child. Every child is different, yet every child is similar in this respect: every child is a glorious gift from above—and with that gift comes immense responsibilities.

Thoughtful parents (like you) understand the critical importance of raising their children with love, with family, with discipline, and with Jesus. By making Jesus a focus in the home, loving moms and dads offer a priceless legacy to their children—a legacy of hope, a legacy of love, and a legacy of eternal life.

Parenting is a full-time job with great responsibilities and the potential for even greater rewards. Your job, as a Christian who's raising a family in this troubled world, is to guide your child lovingly, responsibly, and with a clear focus on Jesus. When you do, the difficult job of parenting will be made a little easier, and your family will be blessed forever.

MORE FROM GOD'S WORD ABOUT CHILDREN

But when Jesus saw this, He was indignant and said to them, "Permit the children to come to Me; do not hinder them; for the kingdom of God belongs to such as these. Truly I say to you, whoever does not receive the kingdom of God like a child will not enter it at all. And He took them in His arms and began blessing them, laying His hands on them.

Mark 10:14-16 NASB

Train a child in the way he should go, and when he is old he will not turn from it.

Proverbs 22:6 NIV

Fix these words of mine in your hearts and minds. Teach them to your children, talking about them when you sit at home and when you walk along the road, when you lie down and when you get up.

Deuteronomy 11:18-19 NIV

When Jesus realized how much this mattered to them, he brought a child to his side. "Whoever accepts this child as if the child were me, accepts me," he said. "And whoever accepts me, accepts the One who sent me. You become great by accepting, not asserting. Your spirit, not your size, makes the difference."

Luke 9:47-48 MSG

MORE IMPORTANT IDEAS ABOUT CHILDREN

Most of us prayed that God would give us children in the first place. Then, we dedicated them to Him soon after they were born. Now, we need to surround them in prayer.

Tim and Beverly LaHaye

A child's life ought to be a child's life, full of simplicity.

Oswald Chambers

Kids really respond to praise and encouragement. I try to praise my kids at least twenty-five times a day.

Josh McDowell

GIVE THANKS EVERY DAY FOR THE HARD JOB OF BEING A PARENT

Raising children is demanding, time-consuming, energy-depleting . . . and profoundly rewarding. Don't ever overlook the rewards.

Kids go where there is excitement.
They stay where there is love.

—

Zig Ziglar

WRITE DOWN YOUR IDEAS ABOUT . . .

Some lessons that you need to teach your children today.

Chapter 8

View Your Parenting Duties as an Exercise in Spiritual Growth

But grow in the grace and knowledge of our Lord and Savior Jesus Christ. To Him be the glory both now and to the day of eternity.

2 Peter 3:18 Holman CSB

TODAY'S BIG IDEA

By your words and by your example, you can help your child grow emotionally and spiritually. And, as responsible parent, that's precisely what you should do.

If you want your child to grow spiritually, you should keep growing, too. And make no mistake: the journey toward spiritual maturity lasts a lifetime.

As Christian parents, we can and should continue to grow in the love and the knowledge of our Savior as long as we live. When we cease to grow, either emotionally or spiritually, we do ourselves and our loved ones a profound disservice. But, if we study God's Word, if we obey His commandments, and if we live in the center of His will, we will not be "stagnant" believers; we will, instead, be growing Christians . . . and that's exactly what God wants for our lives.

Many of life's most important lessons are painful to learn. During times of heartbreak and hardship, God stands ready to protect us. As Psalm 147 promises, "He heals the brokenhearted and bandages their wounds" (NCV). In His own time and according to His master plan, God will heal us if we invite Him into our hearts.

Spiritual growth need not take place only in times of adversity. We should seek to grow in our relationship with the Lord through every season of our lives, through happy times and hard times, through times of celebration and times of pain.

In those quiet moments when we worship God and open our hearts to His Son, the One who made us keeps remaking us. He gives us direction, perspective, wisdom, and courage. And of course, the appropriate moment to accept those spiritual gifts is always the present one.

I've never met anyone who became instantly mature. It's a painstaking process that God takes us through, and it includes such things as waiting, failing, losing, and being misunderstood—each calling for extra doses of perseverance.

Charles Swindoll

MORE FROM GOD'S WORD ABOUT SPIRITUAL GROWTH

For this reason also, since the day we heard this, we haven't stopped praying for you. We are asking that you may be filled with the knowledge of His will in all wisdom and spiritual understanding.

Colossians 1:9 Holman CSB

I want their hearts to be encouraged and joined together in love, so that they may have all the riches of assured understanding, and have the knowledge of God's mystery—Christ.

Colossians 2:2 Holman CSB

Therefore, leaving the elementary message about the Messiah, let us go on to maturity.

Hebrews 6:1 Holman CSB

For You, O God, have tested us; You have refined us as silver is refined. You brought us into the net; You laid affliction on our backs. You have caused men to ride over our heads; we went through fire and through water; but You brought us out to rich fulfillment.

Psalm 66:10–12 NKJV

MORE IMPORTANT IDEAS ABOUT SPIRITUAL GROWTH

As we spend time reading, applying, and obeying our Bibles, the Spirit of Truth Who is also the Spirit of Jesus increasingly reveals Jesus to us.

Anne Graham Lotz

Although God most assuredly wills that His children study Scripture thoroughly, scholarship is not His main goal for us. Relationship is.

Beth Moore

God wants to revolutionize our lives—by showing us how knowing Him can be the most powerful force to help us become all we want to be.

Bill Hybels

THE JOURNEY TOWARD SPIRITUAL MATURITY

Wise parents understand that the quest for spiritual maturity is not a destination to be reached, but a journey—the journey of a lifetime and beyond.

WRITE DOWN YOUR IDEAS ABOUT . . .

What God's Word says about your own spiritual growth.

Part II

Demonstrating Your Faith

As a parent, the most important light you will ever shine is the light that your own life shines on the lives of your children. Proclaiming your faith is never enough—you must also demonstrate it. In Part II, we consider ways to put your faith into action.

Chapter 9

Putting God First in Your Family

Choose for yourselves this day whom
you will serve . . . .
But as for me and my house,
we will serve the Lord.
Joshua 24:15 NKJV

TODAY'S BIG IDEA

As the parent, it's up to you (not your child) to determine the focus of family life at your house. If you and your family members focus on God first, you're on the right track. If you're focused on other things first, it's time to step back and reorder your priorities.

As you fulfill the responsibilities of caring for your family, what is your top priority? Do you and your loved ones strive to place God first in every aspect of your lives, or do you usually focus on other priorities? The answer to this simple question will determine the quality and the direction of your own life and the lives of your family members.

As you contemplate your family's relationship with God and His only begotten Son, remember this: all of mankind is engaged in the practice of worship. Some families choose to worship God and, as a result, they reap the joy that He intends for His children. Other families distance themselves from God by worshiping such things as earthly possessions or personal gratification . . . and when they do so, they suffer.

In the book of Exodus, God warns that we should place no gods before Him (20:3). Yet all too often, we place our Lord in second, third, or fourth place as we worship the gods of pride, possessions, prestige, or power.

When we place our desires for material possessions above our love for the Father—or when we yield to the inevitable temptations and complications of life here in the New Millennium—we find ourselves engaged in a struggle that is similar to the one Jesus faced when He was tempted by Satan. In the wilderness, Satan offered Jesus earthly power and unimaginable riches, but Jesus turned

Satan away and chose instead to worship God. We must do likewise by putting God first and by worshiping only Him.

Does God rule over your heart and your home? Make certain that the honest answer to this question is a resounding yes. In the collective life of every Christian family, God should come first—and it's up to you to make certain that He comes first at your house.

As the first community to which a person is attached and the first authority under which a person learns to live, the family establishes society's most basic values.

Charles Colson

MORE FROM GOD'S WORD ABOUT FAMILY

If a kingdom is divided against itself, that kingdom cannot stand. If a house is divided against itself, that house cannot stand.

Mark 3:24-25 Holman CSB

The one who brings ruin on his household will inherit the wind.

Proverbs 11:29 Holman CSB

Unless the Lord builds a house, its builders labor over it in vain; unless the Lord watches over a city, the watchman stays alert in vain.

Psalm 127:1 Holman CSB

Love must be without hypocrisy. Detest evil; cling to what is good. Show family affection to one another with brotherly love. Outdo one another in showing honor.

Romans 12:9-10 Holman CSB

If I speak the languages of men and of angels, but do not have love, I am a sounding gong or a clanging cymbal.

1 Corinthians 13:1 Holman CSB

MORE IMPORTANT IDEAS ABOUT FAMILY

I like to think of my family as a big, beautiful patchwork quilt—each of us so different yet stitched together by love and life experiences.

Barbara Johnson

God expresses His love by putting us in a family.

Charles Stanley

I cannot overemphasize the importance of parental support and love during the formative years of life. A child's sense of security and well-being is primarily rooted in the stability of his home and family.

James Dobson

PUT GOD WHERE HE BELONGS

Every family puts something or someone in first place. Does God occupy first place in your family? If so, congratulations! If not, it's time to reorder your priorities.

WRITE DOWN YOUR IDEAS ABOUT . . .

What it means to put God first in the life of your family.

Chapter 10

Expressing Your Love

Now these three remain: faith, hope, and love.
But the greatest of these is love.
1 Corinthians 13:13 Holman CSB

TODAY'S BIG IDEA

To a child, a parent's unconditional love serves as a representation of every other kind of love, including God's love. So parental love should be demonstrated with deeds, not just announced with words. Thoughtful parents demonstrate their love by giving their kids heaping helpings of time, attention, discipline, protection, and nurturing.

The familiar words of 1st Corinthians 13 remind us that love is God's commandment. Faith is important, of course. So, too, is hope. But love is more important still. Christ showed His love for us on the cross, and, as Christians, we are called upon to return Christ's love by sharing it. We are commanded (not advised, not encouraged . . . commanded!) to love one another just as Christ loved us (John 13:34). That's a tall order, but as Christians, we are obligated to follow it.

Sometimes love is easy (puppies and sleeping children come to mind), and sometimes love is hard (fallible human beings come to mind). But God's Word is clear: We are to love our families and our neighbors without reservation or condition.

So today and every day, give your child the greatest gift this side of heaven: give your love as you take the time to share Christ's message by word and by example. And, of course, the greatest of these is example.

MORE FROM GOD'S WORD ABOUT LOVE

I pray that you, being rooted and firmly established in love, may be able to comprehend with all the saints what is the breadth and width, height and depth, and to know the Messiah's love that surpasses knowledge, so you may be filled with all the fullness of God.

Ephesians 3:17-19 Holman CSB

If I speak the languages of men and of angels, but do not have love, I am a sounding gong or a clanging cymbal.

1 Corinthians 13:1 Holman CSB

We love because He first loved us.

1 John 4:19 Holman CSB

Dear friends, if God loved us in this way, we also must love one another.

1 John 4:11 Holman CSB

Hatred stirs up conflicts, but love covers all offenses.

Proverbs 10:12 Holman CSB

MORE IMPORTANT IDEAS ABOUT LOVE

Our children don't need a buddy. They need a parent. Sometimes we have to be willing to love our children more than we're desperate for them to like us.

Beth Moore

I see small children as vulnerable little creatures who need buckets of love and tenderness every day of their lives.

James Dobson

From the time I was a very small girl, I knew that my mother and daddy loved each other. It was obvious.

Gigi Graham Tchividjian

PARENTAL LOVE IN ACTION

Of course it's good to tell your kids how you feel about them, but that's not enough. You should also show your children how you feel with your good deeds and your kind words.

WRITE DOWN YOUR IDEAS ABOUT . . .

Ways that you can express your love today.

Chapter 11

Measuring Your Words

A word fitly spoken is like apples of gold
in settings of silver.
Proverbs 25:11 NKJV

TODAY'S BIG IDEA

Words are important. And as a parent, some of the most important words you will ever speak are the words your child hears. So whether you're talking about Jesus or just about anything else, for that matter, choose your words carefully because you can be sure that your youngster is listening very carefully.

How important are the words we speak? More important than we may realize, especially if we're serious about leading our children to Christ. Our words have echoes that extend beyond place or time. If our words are encouraging, we can lift others up; if our words are hurtful, we can hold others back.

So, Mom or Dad, here's a question for you to consider: Are you really trying to be a source of encouragement to all the people you encounter every day, starting with the people who live under your roof? And, are you careful to speak words that lift those people up? If so, you will avoid angry outbursts. You will refrain from impulsive outpourings. You will terminate tantrums. Instead, you will speak words of encouragement and hope to children, to friends, to family members, to coworkers, and even to strangers. And by the way, all the aforementioned people have at least one thing in common: they, like just about everybody else in the world, need all the hope and encouragement they can get.

MORE FROM GOD'S WORD ABOUT THE IMPORTANCE OF THE WORDS YOU SPEAK

For the one who wants to love life and to see good days must keep his tongue from evil and his lips from speaking deceit.

1 Peter 3:10 Holman CSB

Avoid irreverent, empty speech, for this will produce an even greater measure of godlessness.

2 Timothy 2:16 Holman CSB

Pleasant words are a honeycomb: sweet to the taste and health to the body.

Proverbs 16:24 Holman CSB

If anyone thinks he is religious, without controlling his tongue but deceiving his heart, his religion is useless.

James 1:26 Holman CSB

Finally, all of you be of one mind, having compassion for one another; love as brothers, be tenderhearted, be courteous.

1 Peter 3:8 NKJV

MORE IMPORTANT IDEAS ABOUT THE IMPORTANCE OF THE WORDS YOU SPEAK

When you talk, choose the very same words that you would use if Jesus were looking over your shoulder. Because He is.

Marie T. Freeman

Words. Do you fully understand their power? Can any of us really grasp the mighty force behind the things we say? Do we stop and think before we speak, considering the potency of the words we utter?

Joni Eareckson Tada

WORDS MATTER

The words you speak will help shape the kids you love . . . and once you speak those words, you cannot "un-speak" them. Even if you're not speaking directly to your kids, you can be sure that your kids are listening, so choose your words carefully.

WRITE DOWN YOUR IDEAS ABOUT . . .

The impact that your words have upon your children.

Chapter 12

Living Your Faith

Set an example of good works yourself,
with integrity and dignity in your teaching.
Titus 2:7 Holman CSB

TODAY'S BIG IDEA

Your life is a sermon: preach and teach accordingly. The sermons you live are far more important than the ones you preach. Make no mistake, your kids are watching carefully and learning constantly.

It would be very easy to teach our kids everything they need to know about Jesus if we could teach them with words alone. But we can't. Our kids hear some of the things we say, but they watch everything that we do.

What kind of example are you? Are you the kind of parent whose life serves as a powerful example of righteousness? Are you a parent whose behavior serves as a positive role model for your youngsters? Are you the kind of parent whose actions, day in and day out, are based upon integrity, patience, fidelity, and a love for the Lord? If so, you are not only blessed by God, but you are also a powerful force for good in a world that desperately needs positive influences such as yours.

As parents, we serve as unforgettable role models for our children. The lives we lead and the choices we make should serve as enduring examples of the spiritual abundance that is available to all who worship God and obey His commandments.

Are you God's obedient servant? Is your faith in Christ clearly demonstrated by the example that you set for your children? If so, you will be blessed by God, and so, of course, will they.

Phillips Brooks advised, "Be such a man, and live such a life, that if every man were such as you, and every life a life like yours, this earth would be God's Paradise." And that's sound advice because our families and friends are watching . . . and so, for that matter, is God.

Living life with a consistent spiritual walk deeply influences those we love most.

Vonette Bright

MORE FROM GOD'S WORD ABOUT THE IMPORTANCE OF SETTING A GOOD EXAMPLE

You should be an example to the believers in speech, in conduct, in love, in faith, in purity.

1 Timothy 4:12 Holman CSB

Therefore since we also have such a large cloud of witnesses surrounding us, let us lay aside every weight and the sin that so easily ensnares us, and run with endurance the race that lies before us.

Hebrews 12:1 Holman CSB

For the kingdom of God is not in talk but in power.

1 Corinthians 4:20 Holman CSB

Lead a tranquil and quiet life in all godliness and dignity.

1 Timothy 2:2 Holman CSB

For this very reason, make every effort to supplement your faith with goodness, goodness with knowledge, knowledge with self-control, self-control with endurance, endurance with godliness.

2 Peter 1:5-6 Holman CSB

MORE IMPORTANT IDEAS ABOUT THE IMPORTANCE OF SETTING A GOOD EXAMPLE

When it comes to parenting, you can't really teach it if you won't really live it.

Jim Gallery

If you want to teach your child what it means to be a joyful Christian . . . be one.

Marie T. Freeman

In our faith we follow in someone's steps. In our faith we leave footprints to guide others. It's the principle of discipleship.

Max Lucado

WORDS ARE NEVER ENOUGH

When it comes to teaching our children the most important lessons, the things we say pale in comparison to the things we do. Being a responsible parent is a big job, but don't fret: you and God, working together, can handle it!

WRITE DOWN YOUR IDEAS ABOUT . . .

Things you can do today to be a worthy example to your children.

Chapter 13

Demonstrating Parental Love That Reflects God's Love

For the Lord is good, and His love is eternal;
His faithfulness endures through all generations.
Psalm 100:5 Holman CSB

TODAY'S BIG IDEA

Children form their ideas about God's love by experiencing their parents' love. So live—and love—accordingly.

The words of 1 John 4:8 teach us that "He who does not love does not know God, for God is love" (NKJV). And because we can be assured that God is love, we can also be assured that God's heart is a loving heart.

God loves you and your family. He loves you more than you can imagine; His affection is deeper than you can fathom. God made you in His own image and gave you salvation through the person of His Son Jesus Christ. When you accept the love that flows from the heart of God, you are transformed. When you embrace God's love, you feel differently about yourself, your child, your neighbors, your community, your church, and your world. When you open your heart to God's love, you will feel compelled to share God's message—and the story of His only begotten Son—with others.

Corrie ten Boom observed, "We must mirror God's love so we may show Jesus by our lives." And her words most certainly apply to every Christian family, including yours. God's heart is overflowing with love for you and yours. Accept that love. Return that love. Respect that love. And share that love. Today.

MORE FROM GOD'S WORD ABOUT GOD'S LOVE

[Because of] the Lord's faithful love we do not perish, for His mercies never end. They are new every morning; great is Your faithfulness!

Lamentations 3:22-23 Holman CSB

Help me, Lord my God; save me according to Your faithful love.

Psalm 109:26 Holman CSB

Whoever is wise will observe these things, and they will understand the lovingkindness of the Lord.

Psalm 107:43 NKJV

The Lord is gracious and compassionate, slow to anger and great in faithful love. The Lord is good to everyone; His compassion [rests] on all He has made.

Psalm 145:8-9 Holman CSB

God is love, and the one who remains in love remains in God, and God remains in him.

1 John 4:16 Holman CSB

MORE IMPORTANT IDEAS ABOUT GOD'S LOVE

The life of faith is a daily exploration of the constant and countless ways in which God's grace and love are experienced.

Eugene Peterson

Though our feelings come and go, God's love for us does not.

C. S. Lewis

The crux of the matter is not relying on your degree of love for God for stability and security. The prescription to a steady, progressive walk of faith is focusing on God's love for you.

Charles Swindoll

MAKE SURE THEY KNOW WHAT YOU KNOW

You know that "God is love." Now, it's your responsibility to make certain that your children know it, too.

Everything I possess of any worth
is a direct product of God's love.

Beth Moore

WRITE DOWN YOUR IDEAS ABOUT . . .

What God's love means to you and your family.

Chapter 14

Emphasize the Importance of Worship

But an hour is coming, and is now here, when the true worshipers will worship the Father in spirit and truth. Yes, the Father wants such people to worship Him. God is Spirit, and those who worship Him must worship in spirit and truth.

John 4:23-24 Holman CSB

TODAY'S BIG IDEA

As the parent, you have an important task: deciding when and how your family will worship God. You should weave genuine worship into the fabric of family life by honoring God sincerely and often (not just on Sunday mornings).

How can we lead our children to Christ? A great place to start is by emphasizing the importance of worship. When we show our kids what it means to worship God faithfully and fervently—when we demonstrate what it means to honor God's Son in the presence of fellow believers—we are blessed, as are our kids. But if we fail to worship God, for whatever reason, we forfeit the spiritual gifts that might otherwise be ours.

Some people may tell you that they don't engage in worship. Don't believe them. All of humanity is engaged in worship. The question is not whether we worship, but what we worship. Wise parents choose to worship God while teaching their children to do likewise. And the whole family wins.

We must worship our Heavenly Father, not just with our words, but also with deeds. We must do our best to honor Him, to praise Him, to obey Him, and to follow in the footsteps of His Son seven days a week. As we seek to show our kids what genuine Christianity is all about, we must impress upon them that God comes first. Always first.

MORE FROM GOD'S WORD ABOUT WORSHIP

If anyone is thirsty, he should come to Me and drink!

John 7:37 Holman CSB

So that at the name of Jesus every knee should bow—of those who are in heaven and on earth and under the earth—and every tongue should confess that Jesus Christ is Lord, to the glory of God the Father.

Philippians 2:10-11 Holman CSB

I rejoiced with those who said to me, "Let us go to the house of the Lord."

Psalm 122:1 Holman CSB

And every day they devoted themselves to meeting together in the temple complex, and broke bread from house to house. They ate their food with gladness and simplicity of heart, praising God and having favor with all the people. And every day the Lord added those being saved to them.

Acts 2:46-47 Holman CSB

MORE IMPORTANT IDEAS ABOUT WORSHIP

If you will not worship God seven days a week, you do not worship Him on one day a week.

A. W. Tozer

To worship Him in truth means to worship Him honestly, without hypocrisy, standing open and transparent before Him.

Anne Graham Lotz

God shows unbridled delight when He sees people acting in ways that honor Him: when He receives worship, when He sees faith demonstrated in the most trying of circumstances, and when He sees tender love shared among His people.

Bill Hybels

MAKE CHURCH A CELEBRATION, NOT AN OBLIGATION

Your attitude towards church will help determine your kid's attitude toward church . . . so celebrate accordingly!

WRITE DOWN YOUR IDEAS ABOUT . . .

The importance of worship to you and your family.

Chapter 15

DEMONSTRATING CHRISTIAN MATURITY

Flee from youthful passions,
and pursue righteousness, faith, love, and peace,
along with those who call on the Lord
from a pure heart.
2 Timothy 2:22 Holman CSB

TODAY'S BIG IDEA

If you want your youngster to become a mature Christian, then you should realize that your youngster is learning about spiritual maturity from a very important role model: you.

If only your child would always behave maturely and responsibly, parenting would be a breeze. You could talk to your kid about life's most important issues and your youngster would not only listen, but learn. Yet here in the real world, young people don't grow into mature adults overnight . . . and they don't always listen. It takes time for a child to grow up physically, emotionally, and spiritually. So what's a parent to do? Wise parents are patient, loving, encouraging, and understanding. And they pray a lot, too!

So here's a parental prescription that works: let your child grow up at his or her pace, while emphasizing the importance (and the benefit) of behaving responsibly. Put God first, keep talking about Jesus, and make sure that you're the kind of adult—and the kind of parent—that you'd want your child to become.

MORE FROM GOD'S WORD ABOUT MATURITY

Consider it a great joy, my brothers, whenever you experience various trials, knowing that the testing of your faith produces endurance. But endurance must do its complete work, so that you may be mature and complete, lacking nothing.

James 1:2-4 Holman CSB

Brothers, don't be childish in your thinking, but be infants in evil and adult in your thinking.

1 Corinthians 14:20 Holman CSB

But grow in grace, and in the knowledge of our Lord and Saviour Jesus Christ....

2 Peter 3:18 KJV

So teach us to number our days, that we may gain a heart of wisdom.

Psalm 90:12 NKJV

Acquire wisdom—how much better it is than gold! And acquire understanding—it is preferable to silver.

Proverbs 16:16 Holman CSB

MORE IMPORTANT IDEAS ABOUT MATURITY

One of the marks of Spiritual maturity is a consistent, Spirit-controlled life.

Vonette Bright

Salvation is the process that's done, that's secure, that no one can take away from you. Sanctification is the lifelong process of being changed from one degree of glory to the next, growing in Christ, putting away the old, taking on the new.

Max Lucado

I'm not what I want to be. I'm not what I'm going to be. But, thank God, I'm not what I was!

Gloria Gaither

TEACHING VALUES

Your children will learn about life from many sources; the most important source can and should be you. But remember that the lectures you give are never as important as the ones you live.

We have always needed old people
to keep things from going too fast
and young people to keep them
from going too slow. Youth has fire,
and age has light, and we need both.

—

Vance Havner

WRITE DOWN YOUR IDEAS ABOUT . . .

Ways that you can help your child mature.

Part III

Preparing Your Child

As a Christian parent, it's your job to make sure that your youngster has a basic understanding of God's love and God's Son. The lessons in Part III are intended to help you train your child in a number of essential Biblical truths.

Chapter 16

Studying God's Word with Your Child

But He answered, "It is written:
Man must not live on bread alone, but on
every word that comes from the mouth of God."
Matthew 4:4 Holman CSB

TODAY'S BIG IDEA

Our children will learn about Jesus at church and, in some cases, at school. But, the ultimate responsibility for religious teachings should never be delegated to institutions outside the home. As parents, we must teach our children about the love and grace of Jesus Christ by our words and by our actions.

God's wisdom is found in a book like no other: the Holy Bible. The Bible is a roadmap for life here on earth and for life eternal. As Christians, we are called upon to study God's Holy Word, to trust His Word, to follow its commandments, and to share its Good News with the world and with our families. As Christian parents, we must study the Bible, we must meditate upon its meaning, and we must share God's message with our children. Otherwise, we deprive ourselves and our kids of a priceless gift from our Creator.

Warren Wiersbe observed, "When the child of God looks into the Word of God, he sees the Son of God. And, he is transformed by the Spirit of God to share in the glory of God." God's Holy Word is, indeed, a transforming, life-changing, one-of-a-kind treasure. And, a passing acquaintance with the Good Book is insufficient for Christian families that seek to obey God's Word and to understand His will. After all, neither man, nor parents, nor their children should live by bread alone . . .

MORE FROM GOD'S WORD ABOUT GOD'S WORD

Heaven and earth will pass away, but My words will never pass away.

Matthew 24:35 Holman CSB

But the word of the Lord endures forever. And this is the word that was preached as the gospel to you.

1 Peter 1:25 Holman CSB

All Scripture is inspired by God and is profitable for teaching, for rebuking, for correcting, for training in righteousness, so that the man of God may be complete, equipped for every good work.

2 Timothy 3:16-17 Holman CSB

For the word of God is living and effective and sharper than any two-edged sword, penetrating as far as to divide soul, spirit, joints, and marrow; it is a judge of the ideas and thoughts of the heart.

Hebrews 4:12 Holman CSB

The one who is from God listens to God's words. This is why you don't listen, because you are not from God.

John 8:47 Holman CSB

MORE IMPORTANT IDEAS ABOUT GOD'S WORD

Walking in faith brings you to the Word of God. There you will be healed, cleansed, fed, nurtured, equipped, and matured.

Kay Arthur

The only way we can understand the Bible is by personal contact with the Living Word.

Oswald Chambers

There is no way to draw closer to God unless you are in the Word of God every day. It's your compass. Your guide. You can't get where you need to go without it.

Stormie Omartian

REGULAR BIBLE STUDY IS ESSENTIAL

How can you teach your children the importance of God's Holy Word? By example. When teaching your child about the Bible, words are fine—but actually studying the Bible is far better.

WRITE DOWN YOUR IDEAS ABOUT . . .

Ways that you can weave God's Word into the fabric of your life.

Chapter 17

Spending Time with Your Child

Love must be without hypocrisy.
Detest evil; cling to what is good.
Show family affection to one another
with brotherly love.
Outdo one another in showing honor.
Romans 12:9-10 Holman CSB

TODAY'S BIG IDEA

The real currency of family life is time, not dollars. Wise parents give generous amounts of time to their youngsters.

It takes lots of time to build a strong bond between a parent and a child. So do yourself and your child a favor: forget about trying to squeeze in a few minutes here or there and calling it "quality time." When it comes to your family, you'll have a hard time getting quality if you don't insist upon quantity, too.

Every child is different, but every child is similar in this respect: he or she wants and needs plenty of family time (whether he or she is willing to admit it, or not). And make no mistake—parents (unlike you) who try to "farm out" their kids to the care of "hired hands" are making a big mistake. The responsibility of building any family lies squarely on the shoulders of the parents, period.

Do you want to be the kind of parent your kids deserve? Then give them plenty of time—your time. Don't be satisfied to give your kids the scraps that are left from the main course of your day. Give your children the gift of fully-involved, non-diluted, pure, 100% time. Accept no substitutes—because your kids won't.

MORE IMPORTANT IDEAS ABOUT FAMILY

When God asks someone to do something for Him entailing sacrifice, He makes up for it in surprising ways. Though He has led Bill all over the world to preach the gospel, He has not forgotten the little family in the mountains of North Carolina.

Ruth Bell Graham

A family altar can alter a family.

Anonymous

MINIMIZE DISTRACTIONS

There is an important difference between spending time with your children and simply occupying space with them; recognize the difference and take appropriate action. For starters, turn off the television set. Then, take whatever steps are necessary to capture the attention of your children. Today's world is full of distractions for kids and adults alike. Minimize them.

WRITE DOWN YOUR IDEAS ABOUT . . .

What God's Word says about your child's spiritual growth.

Chapter 18

Watching for Teachable Moments

Train up a child in the way he should go,
and when he is old he will not depart from it.
Proverbs 22:6 NKJV

TODAY'S BIG IDEA

As a parent, you are your child's most important teacher. Whether you realize it or not, you are constantly teaching your youngster lessons about life, love, family, and faith. What your youngster learns about Jesus—and what it means to follow in His footsteps—will be learned, first and foremost, at home.

As Christian parents, we want to lead our youngsters to Christ. And we want to share God's wisdom with our children—but we cannot impart what we don't possess. So it's never enough to talk about God's Son; we must also be willing to give Him our lives and our hearts, without reservation. When we do, we can teach our children using both proclamations and (more importantly) demonstrations.

When are the best times to teach your youngster? Deuteronomy 6:7 instructs you to share God's truths, "When you sit in your house and when you walk along the road, when you lie down and when you get up" (Holman CSB). In other words, you should be ready to share God's promises at any time: during regular family gatherings (mealtimes, weekends, holidays, etc.) as well as those unplanned "teachable" moments that seem to pop up from time to time.

At what age should you begin teaching your child about Jesus? As soon as possible. While God's grace can transform a person at any age, wise parents begin teaching their youngsters from the cradle onward.

MORE FROM GOD'S WORD ABOUT TEACHING

Set an example of good works yourself, with integrity and dignity in your teaching.

Titus 2:7 Holman CSB

According to the grace given to us, we have different gifts: If prophecy, use it according to the standard of faith; if service, in service; if teaching, in teaching; if exhorting, in exhortation; giving, with generosity; leading, with diligence; showing mercy, with cheerfulness.

Romans 12:6-8 Holman CSB

The heart of the wise teaches his mouth, and adds learning to his lips.

Proverbs 16:23 NKJV

Be conscientious about yourself and your teaching; persevere in these things, for by doing this you will save both yourself and your hearers.

1 Timothy 4:13 Holman CSB

Light shines on the godly, and joy on those who do right. May all who are godly be happy in the Lord and praise his holy name.

Psalm 97:11-12 NLT

MORE IMPORTANT IDEAS ABOUT TEACHING

Training is not telling, not teaching, not commanding, but something higher than all of these. It is not only telling a child what to do, but it is also showing him how to do it and seeing that it is done.

Andrew Murray

Their little minds had a thousand hands reaching and grabbing for everything they could see (not unlike their physical hands). A parent-teacher's job is to guide as much as possible what the hands of their minds grab and store.

Beth Moore

TEACHING TAKES TIME

Helping our children understand the fundamental truths of Jesus requires time, and lots of it. Our children are always learning. As parents, we must ensure that they are learning from us.

Please teach your kids to work.
You doom them to a life of frustration and
mediocrity if they don't learn
a work ethic from you.

Dave Ramsey

WRITE DOWN YOUR IDEAS ABOUT . . .

Some lessons that you need to teach your children today.

Chapter 19

TALKING ABOUT THE MIRACLE OF CHRISTMAS

But the angel said to them, "Do not be afraid, for you see, I announce to you good news of great joy that will be for all the people: because today in the city of David was born for you a Savior, who is Christ the Lord."

Luke 2:10-11 Holman CSB

TODAY'S BIG IDEA

Christmas is a holiday. Christ's birth is a miracle. We should always focus on the miracle, not the holiday.

For young children, Christmas is, perhaps, the most exciting time of the year. But wise parents never wait until December 25th to celebrate the birth of Jesus. Thoughtful moms and dads talk about Christ's birth—and celebrate it—all throughout the year.

God sent His Son to transform the world and to save it. The Christ Child was born in the most humble of circumstances: in a nondescript village, to parents of simple means, far from the seats of earthly power.

God sent His Son, not as a conqueror or a king, but as an innocent babe. Jesus came, not to be served, but to serve. Jesus did not preach a message of retribution or revenge; He spoke words of compassion and forgiveness. We must do our best to imitate Him.

In the second chapter of Luke, we read about shepherds who were tending their flocks on the night Christ was born. May we, like those shepherds of old, leave our own fields—wherever they may be—and join hands with our children to worship God's priceless gift: His only begotten Son.

MORE IMPORTANT IDEAS ABOUT THE BIRTH OF JESUS

Jesus' birth, too, was greeted by the aging eyes of Zachariah (Luke 2:25-38)—those whose wrinkles betrayed a faith still young and vibrant—trust that never had much use for getting old and cynical.

Calvin Miller

The miracle of Christmas is not on 34th Street; it's in Bethlehem.

Rick Warren

Christmas is about a baby, born in a stable, who changed the world forever.

John Maxwell

TEACHING THE REAL MEANING OF CHRISTMAS

Popular culture encourages mixed messages about Christmas. As a Christian parent, your message must not be mixed; you must focus on the birth of Jesus.

THE BIRTH OF JESUS

And it came to pass in those days that a decree went out from Caesar Augustus that all the world should be registered. This census first took place while Quirinius was governing Syria. So all went to be registered, everyone to his own city. Joseph also went up from Galilee, out of the city of Nazareth, into Judea, to the city of David, which is called Bethlehem, because he was of the house and lineage of David, to be registered with Mary, his betrothed wife, who was with child. So it was, that while they were there, the days were completed for her to be delivered. And she brought forth her firstborn Son, and wrapped Him in swaddling cloths, and laid Him in a manger, because there was no room for them in the inn. Now there were in the same country shepherds living out in the fields, keeping watch over their flock by night.

And behold, an angel of the Lord stood before them, and the glory of the Lord shone around them, and they were greatly afraid. Then the angel said to them, "Do not be afraid, for behold, I bring you good tidings of great joy which will be to all people. For there is born to you this day in the city of David a Savior, who is Christ the Lord. And this will be the sign to you: You will find a Babe wrapped in swaddling cloths, lying in a manger." And suddenly there was with the angel a multitude of the heavenly host praising God and saying: "Glory to God in the highest, And on earth peace, goodwill toward men!"

Luke 2:1-14 NKJV

WRITE DOWN YOUR IDEAS ABOUT . . .

The importance of talking to your child about Jesus.

Chapter 20

Talking About the Life of Jesus

For I have given you an example that you also should do just as I have done for you.

John 13:15 Holman CSB

TODAY'S BIG IDEA

It's good to talk about Jesus. So family discussions about God and His Son shouldn't be reserved for "special" occasions or Sunday School lessons. Since you're serious about your faith, talk to your kids about it. And when it comes to the marvelous things God has done, speak openly, sincerely, and often.

He was the Son of God, but He wore a crown of thorns. He was the Savior of mankind, yet He was put to death on a rough-hewn cross. He offered His healing touch to an unsaved world, and yet the same hands that had healed the sick and raised the dead were pierced with nails.

Jesus Christ, the Son of God, was born into humble circumstances. He walked this earth, not as a ruler of men, but as the Savior of mankind. His crucifixion, a torturous punishment that was intended to end His life and His reign, instead became the pivotal event in the history of all humanity. Christ sacrificed His life on the cross so that we might have eternal life. This gift, freely given by God's only begotten Son, is the priceless possession of everyone who accepts Him as Lord and Savior.

Why did Christ endure the humiliation and torture of the cross? He did it for you; He did it for your child; and He did it for the world. His love is as near as your next breath, as personal as your next thought, more essential than your next heartbeat. And what must you do in response to the Savior's gifts? You must accept His love, praise His name, and share His message of salvation. And, you must conduct yourself in a manner that demonstrates to all the world that your acquaintance with the Master is not a passing fancy but that it is, instead, the cornerstone and the touchstone of your life.

Jesus was the perfect reflection
of God's nature in every situation
He encountered during
His time here on earth.

—

Bill Hybels

MORE FROM GOD'S WORD ABOUT CHRIST'S LOVE

I am the good shepherd. The good shepherd lays down his life for the sheep.

John 10:11 NIV

Just as the Father has loved Me, I also have loved you. Remain in My love.

John 15:9 Holman CSB

Who will separate us from the love of Christ? Will tribulation, or distress, or persecution, or famine, or nakedness, or peril, or sword? But in all these things we overwhelmingly conquer through Him who loved us.

Romans 8:35, 37 NASB

And I am convinced that nothing can ever separate us from his love. Whether we are high above the sky or in the deepest ocean, nothing in all creation will ever be able to separate us from the love of God that is revealed in Christ Jesus our Lord.

Romans 8:38–39 NLT

And remember, I am with you always, to the end of the age.

Matthew 28:20 Holman CSB

MORE IMPORTANT IDEAS ABOUT CHRIST'S LIFE

Jesus was the Savior who would deliver them not only from the bondage of sin but also from meaningless wandering through life.

Anne Graham Lotz

Jesus came into the world so we could know, once and for all, that God is concerned about the way we live, the way we believe, and the way we die.

Billy Graham

Had Jesus been the Word become word, He would have spun theories about life, but since He was the Word become flesh, He put shoes on all His theories and made them walk.

E. Stanley Jones

JESUS: THE LIGHT OF YOUR FAMILY

Jesus is the light of the world. As a caring parent, it's up to you to make certain that He's the light of your family, too.

WRITE DOWN YOUR IDEAS ABOUT . . .

The importance of talking to your child about Christ's life.

Chapter 21

Talking About the Reason Jesus Lived Among Us

For the Son of Man has come to save that which was lost.

Matthew 18:11 NKJV

TODAY'S BIG IDEA

Jesus came to life with a clear purpose: to save those who are lost. As a parent, it's up to you to make sure that your child understands why Jesus was born, why He lived, why He was crucified, and why He was resurrected.

It's important for your child to understand that Christ came to this earth for a purpose: to redeem the world and offer eternal life to those who welcome Him into their hearts. This message, the Good News of God's Son, is the foundation of the Christian faith. Jesus died for the sins of humanity, and as we consider His sacrifice on the cross, we should be profoundly humbled.

Christ humbled Himself on the cross; He did it for you, for your child, and for all mankind. He shed His blood and suffered—for you. He endured unspeakable pain for you and yours . . . and He did it with a clear purpose in mind: so that through His sacrifice, the world might receive salvation.

Today, Jesus stands at the door and knocks. He is offering to walk with you and your youngster through this life and throughout all eternity. So as you approach Him today in prayer, think about His sacrifice, His grace, and His purpose. And be humble.

MORE FROM GOD'S WORD ABOUT CHRIST'S SACRIFICE

For Christ also suffered once for sins, the just for the unjust, that He might bring us to God, being put to death in the flesh but made alive by the Spirit.

1 Peter 3:18 NKJV

Everyone has to die once, then face the consequences. Christ's death was also a one-time event, but it was a sacrifice that took care of sins forever. And so, when he next appears, the outcome for those eager to greet him is, precisely, salvation.

Hebrews 9:27-28 MSG

For when we were still without strength, in due time Christ died for the ungodly.

Romans 5:6 NKJV

But God demonstrates His own love toward us, in that while we were still sinners, Christ died for us.

Romans 5:8 NKJV

But as for me, I will never boast about anything except the cross of our Lord Jesus Christ, through whom the world has been crucified to me, and I to the world.

Galatians 6:14 Holman CSB

MORE IMPORTANT IDEAS ABOUT CHRIST'S PURPOSE

Christ is no Moses, no exactor, no giver of laws, but a giver of grace, a Savior; he is infinite mercy and goodness, freely and bountifully given to us.

Martin Luther

It was not for societies or states that Christ died, but for men.

C. S. Lewis

The richest meaning of your life is contained in the idea that Christ loved you enough to give His life for you.

Calvin Miller

SUFFERING ON THE CROSS

Jesus made His sacrifice so that we might have eternal life. As a parent, you must ensure that your youngster understands the profound meaning and the personal implications of Christ's sacrifice.

WRITE DOWN YOUR IDEAS ABOUT . . .

The importance of talking to your child about Christ's purpose.

Chapter 22

Talking About Discipleship

Then Jesus said to His disciples,
"If anyone wants to come with Me,
he must deny himself, take up his cross,
and follow Me."
Matthew 16:24 Holman CSB

TODAY'S BIG IDEA

Jesus has invited you and your child to become His disciples. As a caring Christian parent, you must make sure that your youngster understands the importance of accepting His invitation.

Because Jesus invites us to follow Him, each of us has a choice to make. We can give our hearts to Jesus, or not.

When Jesus addressed His disciples, He warned them that each one must "take up his cross daily and follow me" (Luke 9:23 NIV). Christ's message was clear: in order to follow Him, Christ's disciples must deny themselves and, instead, trust Him completely. Nothing has changed since then.

If we are to be disciples of Christ, we must trust Him and place Him at the very center of our beings. Jesus never comes "next." He is always first.

Do you seek to fulfill God's purpose for your life? And do you want to help your youngster discover his or her purpose as well? Then you and your child must follow Christ by picking up His cross today and every day.

We encouraged, comforted, and implored
each one of you to walk worthy of God,
who calls you into His own kingdom and glory.

1 Thessalonians 2:12 Holman CSB

MORE FROM GOD'S WORD ABOUT DISCIPLESHIP

"Follow Me," Jesus told them, "and I will make you into fishers of men!" Immediately they left their nets and followed Him.

Mark 1:17-18 Holman CSB

You did not choose Me, but I chose you. I appointed you that you should go out and produce fruit, and that your fruit should remain, so that whatever you ask the Father in My name, He will give you.

John 15:16 Holman CSB

But whoever keeps His word, truly in him the love of God is perfected. This is how we know we are in Him: the one who says he remains in Him should walk just as He walked.

1 John 2:5-6 Holman CSB

The one who loves his life will lose it, and the one who hates his life in this world will keep it for eternal life. If anyone serves Me, he must follow Me. Where I am, there My servant also will be. If anyone serves Me, the Father will honor him.

John 12:25-26 Holman CSB

MORE IMPORTANT IDEAS ABOUT DISCIPLESHIP

Discipleship is a daily discipline: we follow Jesus a step at a time, a day at a time.

Warren Wiersbe

We cannot make disciples of others unless we are disciples ourselves.

Oswald Chambers

There is not Christianity without a cross, for you cannot be a disciple of Jesus without taking up your cross.

Henry Blackaby

REAL DISCIPLESHIP

Talk is cheap. Real ministry has legs. When it comes to discipleship, make sure that your family backs up its words with deeds.

WRITE DOWN YOUR IDEAS ABOUT . . .

Things that you can do today to become
a better disciple.

Chapter 23

Sharing the Story of Christ's Love

For I am persuaded that neither death nor life,
nor angels nor principalities nor powers,
nor things present nor things to come, nor height
nor depth, nor any other created thing,
shall be able to separate us from the love of God
which is in Christ Jesus our Lord.
Romans 8:38-39 NKJV

TODAY'S BIG IDEA

Through His sacrifice on the cross, Jesus demonstrated His love for you and your child. As a responsible parent, it's up to you to make certain your youngster understands that Christ's love changes everything.

As a parent, it's your responsibility to remind your child (and keep reminding you child) how much Jesus loves the people of this world. And how much, exactly, does Christ love us? More than we, as mere mortals, can comprehend. His love is perfect and steadfast. Even though we are fallible and wayward, the Good Shepherd cares for us still. Even though we have fallen far short of the Father's commandments, Christ loves us with a power and depth that are beyond our understanding. The sacrifice that Jesus made upon the cross was made for each of us, and His love endures to the edge of eternity and beyond.

Christ's love changes everything. When you and your family members accept His gift of grace, you are transformed, not only for today, but also for all eternity. If you haven't already done so, accept Jesus Christ as your Savior. And make sure that you've invited your youngster to do the same. Your Savior is waiting patiently for you and your loved ones to invite Him into your heart. Please don't make Him wait a single minute longer.

MORE FROM GOD'S WORD ABOUT CHRIST'S LOVE

I am the good shepherd. The good shepherd lays down his life for the sheep.

John 10:11 Holman CSB

But God proves His own love for us in that while we were still sinners Christ died for us!

Romans 5:8 Holman CSB

Just as the Father has loved Me, I also have loved you. Remain in My love.

John 15:9 Holman CSB

Who can separate us from the love of Christ? Can affliction or anguish or persecution or famine or nakedness or danger or sword? . . . No, in all these things we are more than victorious through Him who loved us.

Romans 8:35, 37 Holman CSB

No one has greater love than this, that someone would lay down his life for his friends.

John 15:13 Holman CSB

MORE IMPORTANT IDEAS ABOUT CHRIST'S LOVE

Christ is like a river that is continually flowing. There are always fresh supplies of water coming from the fountain-head, so that a man may live by it and be supplied with water all his life. So Christ is an ever-flowing fountain; he is continually supplying his people, and the fountain is not spent. They who live upon Christ may have fresh supplies from him for all eternity; they may have an increase of blessedness that is new, and new still, and which never will come to an end.

Jonathan Edwards

Labels, labels, labels. I'm glad Jesus referred to people as people. He never mentioned His friend being a coward, He simply called him Peter. He never referred to the woman who loved him deeply as a prostitute, He just called her Mary Magdalene.

Joni Eareckson Tada

No man ever loved like Jesus.
He taught the blind to see
and the dumb to speak.
He died on the cross to save us.
He bore our sins.
And now God says,
"Because He did, I can forgive you."

Billy Graham

GIVE THANKS FOR HIS LOVE

Today and every day, give thanks for Christ's sacrifice . . . it is the ultimate expression of His love for you.

WRITE DOWN YOUR IDEAS ABOUT . . .

The importance of talking to your child about Christ's love.

Chapter 24

Talking About the Miracle of Easter

"He is not here, but He has been resurrected!"

Luke 24:6 Holman CSB

TODAY'S BIG IDEA

The empty tomb is essential to the Christian faith. So don't wait until Easter to talk about the resurrection. Make sure your youngster understands that the gift of eternal life is the direct result of Christ's sacrifice on the cross and His victory over death.

As Christian parents, we shouldn't wait until Easter to talk to our children about the miracle of the empty tomb. We should talk about Christ's victory over death much more often than that.

When we consider the resurrection of Christ, we marvel at God's power, His love, and His mercy. And if God is for us, what can we possibly have to fear? The answer, of course, is that those who have been saved by our living Savior have absolutely nothing to fear.

God's most precious gift, His only Son, went to Calvary as a sacrifice for a sinful world. May we, as believers who have been saved by the blood of Christ, trust the promises of our Savior. And may we honor Him with our words, our deeds, our thoughts, and our prayers—not only today but also throughout all eternity.

THE RESURRECTION

On the first day of the week, very early in the morning, they came to the tomb, bringing the spices they had prepared. They found the stone rolled away from the tomb. They went in but did not find the body of the Lord Jesus. While they were perplexed about this, suddenly two men stood by them in dazzling clothes. So the women were terrified and bowed down to the ground. "Why are you looking for the living among the dead?" asked the men. "He is not here, but He has been resurrected!"

Luke 24:1-6 Holman CSB

MORE IMPORTANT IDEAS ABOUT THE RESURRECTION

The resurrection of Jesus Christ is the power of God to change history and to change lives.

Bill Bright

The world has never been stable. Jesus Himself was born into the cruelest and most unstable of worlds. No, we have babies and keep trusting and living because the Resurrection is true! The Resurrection was not just a one-time event in history; it is a principle built into the very fabric of our beings, a fact reverberating from every cell of creation: Life wins! Life wins!

Gloria Gaither

THE RESURRECTION IS THE FOUNDATION

The resurrection of Jesus is the foundation of the Christian faith—and it should be the foundation of your family's faith, too.

The stone was rolled away from
the tomb not so Jesus could get out,
but so that the world could look in.
His resurrection assures yours.
Because He lives,
you will live forever.

—

Charles Stanley

WRITE DOWN YOUR IDEAS ABOUT . . .

The importance of talking to your child about the reality of eternal life.

Chapter 25

Talking About the Gift of Eternal Life

For God so loved the world, that he gave his only begotten Son, that whosoever believeth in him should not perish, but have everlasting life.

John 3:16 KJV

TODAY'S BIG IDEA

God offers a priceless gift: the gift of eternal life. Make certain that your youngster understands that the right moment to accept God's gift is always the present one.

Eternal life is not an event that begins when we die. Eternal life begins when we invite Jesus into our hearts. The moment we allow Jesus to reign over our hearts, we've already begun our eternal journeys.

As a thoughtful Christian parent, it's important to remind your child that God's plans are not limited to the ups and downs of everyday life. In fact, the ups and downs of the daily grind are, quite often, impossible for us to understand. As mere mortals, our understanding of the present and our visions for the future—like our lives here on earth—are limited. God's vision is not burdened by such limitations: His plans extend throughout all eternity. And we must trust Him even when we cannot understand the particular details of His plan.

So let us praise the Creator for His priceless gift, and let us share the Good News with all who cross our paths. We return our Father's love by accepting His grace and by sharing His message and His love. When we do, we are blessed here on earth and throughout all eternity.

MORE FROM GOD'S WORD ABOUT ETERNAL LIFE

And this is the testimony: God has given us eternal life, and this life is in His Son. The one who has the Son has life. The one who doesn't have the Son of God does not have life. I have written these things to you who believe in the name of the Son of God, so that you may know that you have eternal life.

1 John 5:11-13 Holman CSB

We do not want you to be uninformed, brothers, concerning those who are asleep, so that you will not grieve like the rest, who have no hope. Since we believe that Jesus died and rose again, in the same way God will bring with Him those who have fallen asleep through Jesus.

1 Thessalonians 4:13-14 Holman CSB

In a little while the world will see Me no longer, but you will see Me. Because I live, you will live too.

John 14:19 Holman CSB

MORE IMPORTANT IDEAS ABOUT ETERNAL LIFE

I can still hardly believe it. I, with shriveled, bent fingers, atrophied muscles, gnarled knees, and no feeling from the shoulders down, will one day have a new body—light, bright and clothed in righteousness—powerful and dazzling.

Joni Eareckson Tada

Teach us to set our hopes on heaven, to hold firmly to the promise of eternal life, so that we can withstand the struggles and storms of this world.

Max Lucado

SHARING THE STORY OF GOD'S GRACE

Remember that His grace is enough . . . enough for today and for all eternity. God promises that His grace is sufficient for your needs and your children's needs. Believe Him.

WRITE DOWN YOUR IDEAS ABOUT . . .

The importance of talking to your child about the resurrection.

Part IV

Leading Your Child to Christ

The lessons in Part IV will help you to engage your youngster in discussions about Jesus. These discussions can help you lead your youngster to Christ.

Chapter 26

Welcoming Your Child's Questions

Let the little children come to Me; don't stop them, for the kingdom of God belongs to such as these.

Mark 10:14 Holman CSB

TODAY'S BIG IDEA

If you're a typical parent, you're tempted to lecture your child, but there may be a better way to get your message across. Sometimes, asking the right questions is better than having all the answers.

All children have questions and most children are quick to ask them, especially if parents encourage their kids to ask. Are you the kind of parent who welcomes your youngster's queries? If so, congratulations. If not, perhaps it's time to take a careful look at the way you're communicating (or not communicating) with your kid.

If you're a question-averse parent, perhaps you've been under the misconception that grownups are supposed to have "all the answers." In truth, no parent has the solution to every conceivable question, and it's perfectly okay to make that fact clear to your child. But it's also important to assure your youngster that you have the most important answers to life's most important questions, and that your answers are based upon the unshakable promises found in God's Holy Word.

So the next time your child begins to ask, "Why, why, why?" please don't be too quick to respond with that overused parental retort: "Because I said so, that's why!" Instead of rebuffing your child's questions, welcome them. And do your best to answer them, using the Bible as your guidebook. Of course, you may not be able to answer every question your child can conjure up, but you'll certainly be able to answer the most important ones . . . and that's what really matters.

We must lay our questions,
frustrations, anxieties, and
impotence at the feet of God
and wait for His answer.
And then receiving it,
we must live by faith.

Kay Arthur

MORE FROM GOD'S WORD ABOUT QUESTIONS

We are pressured in every way but not crushed; we are perplexed but not in despair.

2 Corinthians 4:8 Holman CSB

Now if any of you lacks wisdom, he should ask God, who gives to all generously and without criticizing, and it will be given to him. But let him ask in faith without doubting. For the doubter is like the surging sea, driven and tossed by the wind.

James 1:5-6 Holman CSB

But the wisdom from above is first pure, then peace-loving, gentle, compliant, full of mercy and good fruits, without favoritism and hypocrisy.

James 3:17 Holman CSB

No wisdom, no understanding, and no counsel [will prevail] against the Lord.

Proverbs 21:30 Holman CSB

So those who suffer according to God's will should, in doing good, entrust themselves to a faithful Creator.

1 Peter 4:19 Holman CSB

MORE IMPORTANT IDEAS ABOUT QUESTIONS

Be to the world a sign that while we as Christians do not have all the answers, we do know and care about the questions.

Billy Graham

We are finding we don't have such a gnawing need to know the answers when we know the Answer.

Gloria Gaither

We basically have two choices to make in dealing with the mysteries of God. We can wrestle with Him or we can rest in Him.

Calvin Miller

MEANINGFUL MOMENTS CAN COME IN SMALL PACKAGES

You don't have to haul your kid to a deserted island to have a meaningful conversation. Meaningful moments between you and your child can happen anywhere—and it's up to you to make sure that they do.

WRITE DOWN YOUR IDEAS ABOUT . . .

The way that you do respond, and should respond, to your child's questions.

Chapter 27

LISTENING TO YOUR CHILD

A wise man will listen and increase his learning.
Proverbs 1:5 Holman CSB

TODAY'S BIG IDEA

For most parents, the temptation to lecture is great; it takes conscious effort to hold one's tongue until one's ears are fully engaged. When a parent is able to do so, his or her efforts are usually rewarded.

For many parents, the temptation to lecture their children is almost irresistible. But oftentimes, it's more helpful to listen than to lecture.

God's Word instructs us to be quick to listen and slow to speak. And when it comes to the important job of raising the next generation and strengthening our families, we're wise to listen carefully (first) and then offer helpful words (next).

Perhaps God gave us two ears and one mouth for a reason: so that we might listen twice as much as we speak. After all, listening quietly to our kids can be a wonderful form of encouragement. Besides, after we've listened carefully to our youngsters, we're more likely to respond wisely, not impulsively.

So remember that, as a parent, you have the power to guide your child with your words and your ears. And remember that the words you don't speak can be just as helpful as the ones you do speak. So talk—and listen—accordingly.

My dear brothers and sisters,
always be willing to listen
and slow to speak.

James 1:19 NCV

MORE IMPORTANT IDEAS ABOUT LISTENING

Part of good communication is listening with the eyes as well as with the ears.

Josh McDowell

Children just don't fit into a "to do" list very well. It takes time to be an effective parent when children are small. It takes time to introduce them to good books—it takes time to fly kites and play punch ball and put together jigsaw puzzles. It takes time to listen.

James Dobson

IF AT FIRST YOU DON'T SUCCEED, KEEP LISTENING

If your child is uncommunicative, don't give up; continue to listen and keep responding with love and encouragement; in all likelihood, the communication between the two of you will eventually improve.

One of the best ways to encourage
someone who's hurting
is with your ears—by listening.

—

Barbara Johnson

WRITE DOWN YOUR IDEAS ABOUT . . .

Steps that you can take to become a better listener.

Chapter 28

Talking About What It Means to Accept Christ

Therefore if anyone is in Christ,
he is a new creature; the old things passed away;
behold, new things have come.
2 Corinthians 5:17 Holman CSB

TODAY'S BIG IDEA

Accepting Christ is a matter of both the head and the heart. Make sure that your child understands the need to give Him both.

The decision to accept (or to reject) Jesus is the pivotal decision facing you and your child. It is a decision that cannot be ignored. It is a decision that has both earthly and eternal consequences. And it's a decision that each of us must make for ourselves.

It's up to you, a Christian parent, to talk openly to your child about the need to accept God's gift of eternal life, a gift that is freely offered to those who accept God's Son.

Warren Wiersbe observed, "The greatest miracle of all is the transformation of a lost sinner into a child of God." And Oswald Chambers noted, "If the Spirit of God has transformed you within, you will exhibit Divine characteristics in your life, not good human characteristics. God's life in us expresses itself as God's life, not as a human life trying to be godly."

When we invite Christ to reign over our hearts, we become new creations through Him. And we are transformed not just for a day, or for a lifetime, but for all eternity.

MORE FROM GOD'S WORD ABOUT ACCEPTING CHRIST

Yet we know that no one is justified by the works of the law but by faith in Jesus Christ. And we have believed in Christ Jesus, so that we might be justified by faith in Christ and not by the works of the law, because by the works of the law no human being will be justified.

Galatians 2:16 Holman CSB

Whoever believes that Jesus is the Christ is born of God, and everyone who loves Him who begot also loves him who is begotten of Him.

1 John 5:1 NKJV

God wanted to make known to those among the Gentiles the glorious wealth of this mystery, which is Christ in you, the hope of glory.

Colossians 1:27 Holman CSB

And we have seen and testify that the Father has sent the Son as Savior of the world.

1 John 4:14 NKJV

MORE IMPORTANT IDEAS ABOUT ACCEPTING CHRIST

Reconciliation becomes a reality for us when we accept Christ by faith.

Charles Stanley

Ask Christ to come into your heart to forgive you and help you. When you do, Christ will take up residence in your life by His Holy Spirit, and when you face temptations and trials, you will no longer face them alone.

Billy Graham

When once you get into personal contact with Jesus Christ, you will never be the same again.

Oswald Chambers

THE TIME IS NOW

Remind your child that the appropriate moment to let Jesus rule one's heart is always the present moment.

A man can accept what Christ has done
without knowing how it works;
indeed, he certainly won't know how
it works until he's accepted it.

—

C. S. Lewis

WRITE DOWN YOUR IDEAS ABOUT . . .

The importance of talking to your child about accepting Christ.

Chapter 29

Talking About What It Means to Be a Christian

I have spoken these things to you
so that My joy may be in you
and your joy may be complete.
John 15:11 Holman CSB

TODAY'S BIG IDEA

Christianity is more than a way of worshipping; it's a way of life. For believers—Christian parents and children alike—every day should provide opportunities to honor God by walking in the footsteps of His Son.

What is "real" Christianity? Think of it as an ongoing relationship—an all-encompassing relationship with God and with His Son Jesus.

It is inevitable that your life must be lived in relationship to God. The question is not if you will have a relationship with Him; the burning question is whether that relationship will be one that seeks to honor Him or one that seeks to ignore Him.

Your relationship with God is ongoing; it unfolds day by day, and it offers countless opportunities to grow closer to Him . . . or not. As each new day unfolds, you are confronted with a wide range of decisions: how you will behave, where you will direct your thoughts, with whom you will associate, and what you will choose to worship. These choices, along with many others, are yours and yours alone. How you choose determines how your relationship with God will unfold.

All of us, parents and children alike, inhabit a world that discourages heartfelt devotion and obedience to the Creator. Everywhere we turn, or so it seems, we are confronted by a mind-numbing assortment of distractions, temptations, obligations, and frustrations. Yet even on our busiest days, God beckons us to slow down and consult Him. When we do, we avail ourselves of the peace and abundance that only He can give.

Joy is the direct result of having
God's perspective on our daily lives
and the effect of loving our Lord
enough to obey His commands
and trust His promises.

—

Bill Bright

MORE FROM GOD'S WORD ABOUT GOD'S PRESENCE

Draw near to God, and He will draw near to you.

James 4:8 Holman CSB

You will seek Me and find Me when you search for Me with all your heart.

Jeremiah 29:13 Holman CSB

The Lord is near all who call out to Him, all who call out to Him with integrity. He fulfills the desires of those who fear Him; He hears their cry for help and saves them.

Psalm 145:18-19 Holman CSB

Surely goodness and mercy shall follow me all the days of my life: and I will dwell in the house of the Lord for ever.

Psalm 23:6 KJV

I am not alone, because the Father is with Me.

John 16:32 Holman CSB

MORE IMPORTANT IDEAS ABOUT DISCIPLESHIP AND JOY

If you want to teach your child what it means to be a joyful Christian . . . be one.

Marie T. Freeman

Joy is a by-product not of happy circumstances, education or talent, but of a healthy relationship with God and a determination to love Him no matter what.

Barbara Johnson

True happiness and contentment cannot come from the things of this world. The blessedness of true joy is a free gift that comes only from our Lord and Savior, Jesus Christ.

Dennis Swanberg

JOY IS CONTAGIOUS

Remember that a joyful family starts with joyful parents.

WRITE DOWN YOUR IDEAS ABOUT . . .

The importance of talking to your child about the joys of being a Christian.

Chapter 30

A PLAN OF SALVATION

And this is the testimony: God has given us eternal life, and this life is in His Son. The one who has the Son has life. The one who doesn't have the Son of God does not have life.

1 John 5:11-12 Holman CSB

TODAY'S BIG IDEA

Now, after 29 lessons, it's time to talk to your youngster about the plan of salvation. If you're prepared to have that conversation with your child, the following pages can help.

PARENTS: READ THIS PLAN WITH TWEENS, TEENS, AND ADULT CHILDREN

A PLAN OF SALVATION

1. God loves you, and He demonstrated that love by sending His only begotten Son in order that you might have abundance and eternal life.

I am come that they might have life,
and that they might have it more abundantly.
John 10:10 KJV

For God so loved the world, that he gave his
only begotten Son, that whosoever believeth in him should
not perish, but have everlasting life.
John 3:16 KJV

2. You, like all human beings, have sinned. Sin separates you from God. A spiritual rebirth takes place when you turn your life over to Jesus Christ.

For all have sinned and fall short
of the glory of God.
Romans 3:23 Holman CSB

For the wages of sin is death, but the gift of God is eternal life in Christ Jesus our Lord.
Romans 6:23 Holman CSB

3. Salvation is made possible by Christ's death and resurrection.

For Christ also suffered once for sins, the just for the unjust, that He might bring us to God, being put to death in the flesh but made alive by the Spirit.
1 Peter 3:18 NKJV

In Him we have redemption through His blood, the forgiveness of our trespasses, according to the riches of His grace that He lavished on us with all wisdom and understanding.
Ephesians 1:7-8 Holman CSB

4. Salvation becomes yours when you admit that you are a sinner; when you admit that you cannot save yourself, and when you invite Christ to rule over your heart and your life. When you do, you will be "born again."

Therefore repent and turn back,
that your sins may be wiped out.
Acts 3:19 Holman CSB

For by grace you are saved through faith,
and this is not from yourselves; it is God's gift—
not from works, so that no one can boast.
Ephesians 2:8-9 Holman CSB

A SINNER'S PRAYER

Dear Jesus, I am a sinner. But, I believe that You died and
rose from the grave so that I might have eternal life.
Come into my heart, Jesus, take control of my life,
forgive my sins, and save me. I am now placing
my trust in You alone for my salvation,
and I accept Your gift of eternal life.
Amen

PARENTS: READ THIS PLAN WITH YOUNGER CHILDREN

GOD'S PLAN FOR ETERNAL LIFE

1. God loves you, and He showed His love for you by sending the baby Jesus into the world so that, through Him, you might live forever in heaven.

For God so loved the world, that he gave his only begotten Son, that whosoever believeth in him should not perish, but have everlasting life.

John 3:16 KJV

2. No matter how hard you try to be a good person, you still make mistakes—you can never be perfect. Sins separate you from God, but when you invite Jesus into your heart, He wipes away all those sins.

All have sinned and are not good enough for God's glory.

Romans 3:23 NCV

For the wages of sin is death, but the gift of God is eternal life in Christ Jesus our Lord.

Romans 6:23 Holman CSB

3. Jesus wants you to live forever in heaven; that's why He made the sacrifice on the cross.

For Christ also suffered once for sins, the just for the unjust, that He might bring us to God, being put to death in the flesh but made alive by the Spirit.
1 Peter 3:18 NCV

I assure you, anyone who believes in me already has eternal life.
John 6:47 NLT

4. You can't earn your way into heaven. But when you admit your mistakes, and when you invite Jesus into your heart, you'll receive God's amazing gift: the gift of living joyfully in heaven forever.

Therefore repent and turn back, that your sins may be wiped out.
Acts 3:19 Holman CSB

For by grace you are saved through faith, and this is not from yourselves; it is God's gift— not from works, so that no one can boast.
Ephesians 2:8-9 Holman CSB

A PRAYER INVITING JESUS INTO YOUR HEART

Dear Jesus, I make lots of mistakes; no matter how hard I try, I can't be perfect. But, I believe that You died and rose up again so I can live forever in heaven. Come into my heart, Jesus, forgive my sins, lead me every day, and save me. I am now placing my trust in You alone for my salvation, and I accept Your gift of eternal life. Amen

MORE IMPORTANT IDEAS ABOUT SALVATION

If we accept His invitation to salvation, we live with Him forever. However, if we do not accept because we refuse His only Son as our Savior, then we exclude ourselves from My Father's House. It's our choice.

Anne Graham Lotz

In the depths of our sin, Christ died for us. He did not wait for persons to get as close as possible through obedience to the law and righteous living.

Beth Moore

Today is the day of salvation. Some people miss heaven by only eighteen inches—the distance between their heads and their hearts.

Corrie ten Boom

Salvation is not an event; it is a process.

Henry Blackaby

Appendix

LEADING YOUR CHILD TO CHRIST:

A SUMMARY OF KEY PRINCIPLES

A SUMMARY OF THE 30 KEY PRINCIPLES

1. As a Christian parent, you have many important responsibilities. But no responsibility is more important than your duty, as a parent, to lead your child to Christ.

2. Your child's faith will be a direct reflection of your faith. If you want your child's faith to be strong, your faith should be strong, too.

3. If you need help communicating with your child, ask God for His help in finding the right words to say. When you ask Him, sincerely and often, He will answer your prayers.

4. Absolutely no parental duty is more important than the duty of praying for your child.

5. When it comes to the job of teaching your youngster about Jesus, accountability begins with the person you see in the mirror. As a responsible Christian parent, you should tell the story of Jesus clearly, confidently, and often.

6. Simply put, wisdom starts with God. And if you want to convey real wisdom to your young child, you and your youngster should study God's Word together every day.

7. It's hard work being a responsible parent, but the rewards always outweigh the costs. Simply put, your youngster is a marvelous gift from God. And, your opportunity to be a parent is yet another gift, for which you should give thanks.

8. By your words and by your example, you can help your child grow emotionally and spiritually. And, as a responsible parent, that's precisely what you should do.

9. As the parent, it's up to you (not your child) to determine the focus of family life at your house. If you and your family members focus on God first, you're on the right track. If you're focused on other things first, it's time to step back and reorder your priorities.

10. To a child, a parent's unconditional love serves as a representation of every other kind of love, including God's love. So parental love should be

demonstrated with deeds, not just announced with words. Thoughtful parents demonstrate their love by giving their kids heaping helpings of time, attention, discipline, protection, and nurturing.

11. Words are important. And as a parent, some of the most important words you will ever speak are the words your child hears. So whether you're talking about Jesus or just about anything else, for that matter, choose your words carefully because you can be sure that your youngster is listening very carefully.

12. Your life is a sermon: preach and teach accordingly. The sermons you live are far more important than the ones you preach. Make no mistake, your kids are watching carefully and learning constantly.

13. Children form their ideas about God's love by experiencing their parents' love. So live—and love—accordingly.

14. As the parent, you have an important task: deciding when and how your family will worship God. You should weave genuine worship into the fabric of family life by honoring God sincerely and often (not just on Sunday mornings).

15. If you want your youngster to become a mature Christian, then you should realize that your youngster is learning about spiritual maturity from a very important role model: you.

16. Our children will learn about Jesus at church and, in some cases, at school. But, the ultimate responsibility for religious teachings should never be delegated to institutions outside the home. As parents, we must teach our children about the love and grace of Jesus Christ by our words and by our actions.

17. The real currency of family life is time, not dollars. Wise parents give generous amounts of time to their youngsters.

18. As a parent, you are your child's most important teacher. Whether you realize it or not, you are constantly teaching your youngster lessons about life, love, family, and faith. What your youngster learns about Jesus—and what it means to follow in His footsteps—will be learned, first and foremost, at home.

19. Christmas is a holiday. Christ's birth is a miracle. We should always focus on the miracle, not the holiday.

20. It's good to talk about Jesus. So family discussions about God and His Son shouldn't be reserved for "special" occasions or Sunday School lessons. Since you're serious about your faith, talk to your kids about it. And when it comes to the marvelous things God has done, speak openly, sincerely, and often.

21. Jesus came to life with a clear purpose: to save those who are lost. As a parent, it's up to you to make sure that your child understands why Jesus was born, why He lived, why He was crucified, and why He was resurrected.

22. Jesus has invited you and your child to become His disciples. As a caring Christian parent, you must make sure that your youngster understands the importance of accepting His invitation.

23. Through His sacrifice on the cross, Jesus demonstrated His love for you and your child. As a responsible parent, it's up to you to make certain your youngster understands that Christ's love changes everything.

24. The empty tomb is essential to the Christian faith. So don't wait until Easter to talk about the resurrection. Make sure your youngster understands that the gift of eternal life is the direct result of Christ's sacrifice on the cross and His victory over death.

25. God offers a priceless gift: the gift of eternal life. Make certain that your youngster understands that the right moment to accept God's gift is always the present one.

26. If you're a typical parent, you're tempted to lecture your child, but there may be a better way to get your message across. Sometimes, asking the right questions is better than having all the answers.

27. For most parents, the temptation to lecture is great; it takes conscious effort to hold one's tongue until one's ears are fully engaged. When a parent is able to do so, his or her efforts are usually rewarded.

28. Accepting Christ is a matter of both the head and the heart. Make sure that your child understands the need to give Him both.

29. Christianity is more than a way of worshipping; it's a way of life. For believers—Christian parents and children alike—every day should provide opportunities to honor God by walking in the footsteps of His Son.

30. Talk to your youngster about the plan of salvation.

More Verses from God's Word to Share with Your Child

ATTITUDE

Make your own attitude that of Christ Jesus.

Philippians 2:5 Holman CSB

Finally brothers, whatever is true, whatever is honorable, whatever is just, whatever is pure, whatever is lovely, whatever is commendable—if there is any moral excellence and if there is any praise—dwell on these things.

Philippians 4:8 Holman CSB

Let this mind be in you which was also in Christ Jesus, who, being in the form of God, did not consider it robbery to be equal with God, but made Himself of no reputation, taking the form of a bondservant, and coming in the likeness of men. And being found in appearance as a man, He humbled Himself and became obedient to the point of death, even the death of the cross.

Philippians 2:5-8 NKJV

For the word of God is living and powerful, and sharper than any two-edged sword, piercing even to the division of soul and spirit, and of joints and marrow, and is a discerner of the thoughts and intents of the heart.

Hebrews 4:12 NKJV

CHARACTER

Blessed is the man who walks not in the counsel of the ungodly, nor stands in the path of sinners, nor sits in the seat of the scornful; but his delight is in the law of the Lord, and in His law he meditates day and night. He shall be like a tree planted by the rivers of water, that brings forth its fruit in its season, whose leaf also shall not wither; and whatever he does shall prosper.

Psalm 1:1-3 NKJV

People with integrity have firm footing, but those who follow crooked paths will slip and fall.

Proverbs 10:9 NLT

In everything set them an example by doing what is good. In your teaching show integrity, seriousness and soundness of speech that cannot be condemned, so that those who oppose you may be ashamed because they have nothing bad to say about us.

Titus 2:7 NIV

We also have joy with our troubles, because we know that these troubles produce patience. And patience produces character, and character produces hope.

Romans 5:3-4 NCV

COURAGE

Be strong and courageous, and do the work. Don't be afraid or discouraged, for the Lord God, my God, is with you. He won't leave you or forsake you.

1 Chronicles 28:20 Holman CSB

For God has not given us a spirit of fearfulness, but one of power, love, and sound judgment.

2 Timothy 1:7 Holman CSB

Haven't I commanded you: be strong and courageous? Do not be afraid or discouraged, for the Lord your God is with you wherever you go.

Joshua 1:9 Holman CSB

But when Jesus heard it, He answered him, "Don't be afraid. Only believe."

Luke 8:50 Holman CSB

But He said to them, "Why are you fearful, you of little faith?" Then He got up and rebuked the winds and the sea. And there was a great calm.

Matthew 8:26 Holman CSB

Doubts

If you don't know what you're doing, pray to the Father. He loves to help. You'll get his help, and won't be condescended to when you ask for it. Ask boldly, believingly, without a second thought. People who "worry their prayers" are like wind-whipped waves. Don't think you're going to get anything from the Master that way, adrift at sea, keeping all your options open.

James 1:5-8 MSG

Immediately the father of the child cried out and said with tears, "Lord, I believe; help my unbelief!"

Mark 9:24 NKJV

So He said, "Come." And when Peter had come down out of the boat, he walked on the water to go to Jesus. But when he saw that the wind was boisterous, he was afraid; and beginning to sink he cried out, saying, "Lord, save me!" And immediately Jesus stretched out His hand and caught him, and said to him, "O you of little faith, why did you doubt?" And when they got into the boat, the wind ceased.

Matthew 14:29-32 NKJV

Evil

Therefore, submit to God. But resist the Devil, and he will flee from you. Draw near to God, and He will draw near to you. Cleanse your hands, sinners, and purify your hearts, double-minded people!

James 4:7-8 Holman CSB

For everyone who practices wicked things hates the light and avoids it, so that his deeds may not be exposed. But anyone who lives by the truth comes to the light, so that his works may be shown to be accomplished by God.

John 3:20–21 Holman CSB

He replied, "Every plant that My heavenly Father didn't plant will be uprooted."

Matthew 15:13 Holman CSB

But the path of the just is like the shining sun, that shines ever brighter unto the perfect day. The way of the wicked is like darkness; they do not know what makes them stumble.

Proverbs 4:18-19 NKJV

Don't consider yourself to be wise; fear the Lord and turn away from evil.

Proverbs 3:7 Holman CSB

MODERATION

Moderation is better than muscle, self-control better than political power.

Proverbs 16:32 MSG

Add to your faith virtue; and to virtue, knowledge; and to knowledge, temperance; and to temperance, patience; and to patience, godliness; and to godliness, brotherly kindness; and to brotherly kindness, charity.

2 Peter 1:5-7 KJV

An overseer, then, must be above reproach, the husband of one wife, temperate, prudent, respectable, hospitable, able to teach, not addicted to wine or pugnacious, but gentle, peaceable, free from the love of money.

1 Timothy 3:2-3 NASB

I discipline my body and make it my slave.

1 Corinthians 9:27 NASB

No one can serve two masters; for either he will hate the one and love the other, or he will be devoted to one and despise the other. You cannot serve God and wealth.

Matthew 6:24 NASB

Optimism

Make me hear joy and gladness.

Psalm 51:8 NKJV

My cup runs over. Surely goodness and mercy shall follow me all the days of my life; and I will dwell in the house of the Lord Forever.

Psalm 23:5-6 NKJV

But if we hope for what we do not see, we eagerly wait for it with patience.

Romans 8:25 Holman CSB

For God has not given us a spirit of fearfulness, but one of power, love, and sound judgment.

2 Timothy 1:7 Holman CSB

I am able to do all things through Him who strengthens me.

Philippians 4:13 Holman CSB

Peer Pressure

He who walks with wise men will be wise, but the companion of fools will be destroyed.

Proverbs 13:20 NKJV

For am I now trying to win the favor of people, or God? Or am I striving to please people? If I were still trying to please people, I would not be a slave of Christ.

Galatians 1:10 Holman CSB

Stay away from a foolish man; you will gain no knowledge from his speech.

Proverbs 14:7 Holman CSB

My son, if sinners entice you, don't be persuaded.

Proverbs 1:10 Holman CSB

Blessed is the man who walks not in the counsel of the ungodly, nor stands in the path of sinners, nor sits in the seat of the scornful; but his delight is in the law of the Lord, and in His law he meditates day and night.

Psalm 1:1-2 NKJV

Do not be deceived: "Bad company corrupts good morals."

1 Corinthians 15:33 Holman CSB

Praise

Praise the Lord! Oh, give thanks to the Lord, for He is good! For His mercy endures forever.

Psalm 106:1 NKJV

In everything give thanks; for this is the will of God in Christ Jesus for you.

2 Thessalonians 5:18 NKJV

From the rising of the sun to its going down the Lord's name is to be praised.

Psalm 113:3 NKJV

So that at the name of Jesus every knee should bow—of those who are in heaven and on earth and under the earth—and every tongue should confess that Jesus Christ is Lord, to the glory of God the Father.

Philippians 2:10-11 Holman CSB

Enter into His gates with thanksgiving, and into His courts with praise. Be thankful to Him, and bless His name. For the Lord is good; His mercy is everlasting, and His truth endures to all generations.

Psalm 100:4-5 NKJV

PRIORITIES

Don't abandon wisdom, and she will watch over you; love her, and she will guard you.

Proverbs 4:6 Holman CSB

And I pray this: that your love will keep on growing in knowledge and every kind of discernment, so that you can determine what really matters and can be pure and blameless in the day of Christ.

Philippians 1:9 Holman CSB

So teach us to number our days, that we may gain a heart of wisdom.

Psalm 90:12 NKJV

For where your treasure is, there your heart will be also.

Luke 12:34 Holman CSB

He said to them all, "If anyone desires to come after Me, let him deny himself, and take up his cross daily, and follow Me. For whoever desires to save his life will lose it, but whoever loses his life for My sake will save it."

Luke 9:23-24 NKJV

PROBLEMS

Let not your heart be troubled: ye believe in God, believe also in me.

John 14:1 KJV

People who do what is right may have many problems, but the Lord will solve them all.

Psalm 34:19 NCV

Be joyful because you have hope. Be patient when trouble comes, and pray at all times.

Romans 12:12 NCV

I have told you these things, so that in me you may have peace. In this world you will have trouble. But take heart! I have overcome the world.

John 16:33 NIV

When troubles come and all these awful things happen to you, in future days you will come back to God, your God, and listen obediently to what he says. God, your God, is above all a compassionate God. In the end he will not abandon you, he won't bring you to ruin, he won't forget the covenant with your ancestors which he swore to them.

Deuteronomy 4:30-31 MSG

SELF-ESTEEM

For You have made him a little lower than the angels, And You have crowned him with glory and honor.

Psalm 8:5 NKJV

How happy are those whose way is blameless, who live according to the law of the Lord! Happy are those who keep His decrees and seek Him with all their heart.

Psalm 119:1-2 Holman CSB

Happy is the one whose help is the God of Jacob, whose hope is in the Lord his God.

Psalm 146:5 Holman CSB

If God is for us, who is against us?

Romans 8:31 Holman CSB

Finally, brethren, whatever things are true, whatever things are noble, whatever things are just, whatever things are pure, whatever things are lovely, whatever things are of good report, if there is any virtue and if there is anything praiseworthy—meditate on these things.

Philippians 4:8 NKJV

For God so loved the world,
that he gave his only begotten Son,
that whosoever believeth in him
should not perish,
but have everlasting life.

John 3:16 KJV